This book belongs to:
(Write your name in the palms of my hands)

I thank God my name is written on the palms of His hands . . . -- Isaiah 49:16 (NLT)

The Worker Bees

Adapted from
The Parable Of The Workers In The Vineyard
from The Gospel Of Matthew

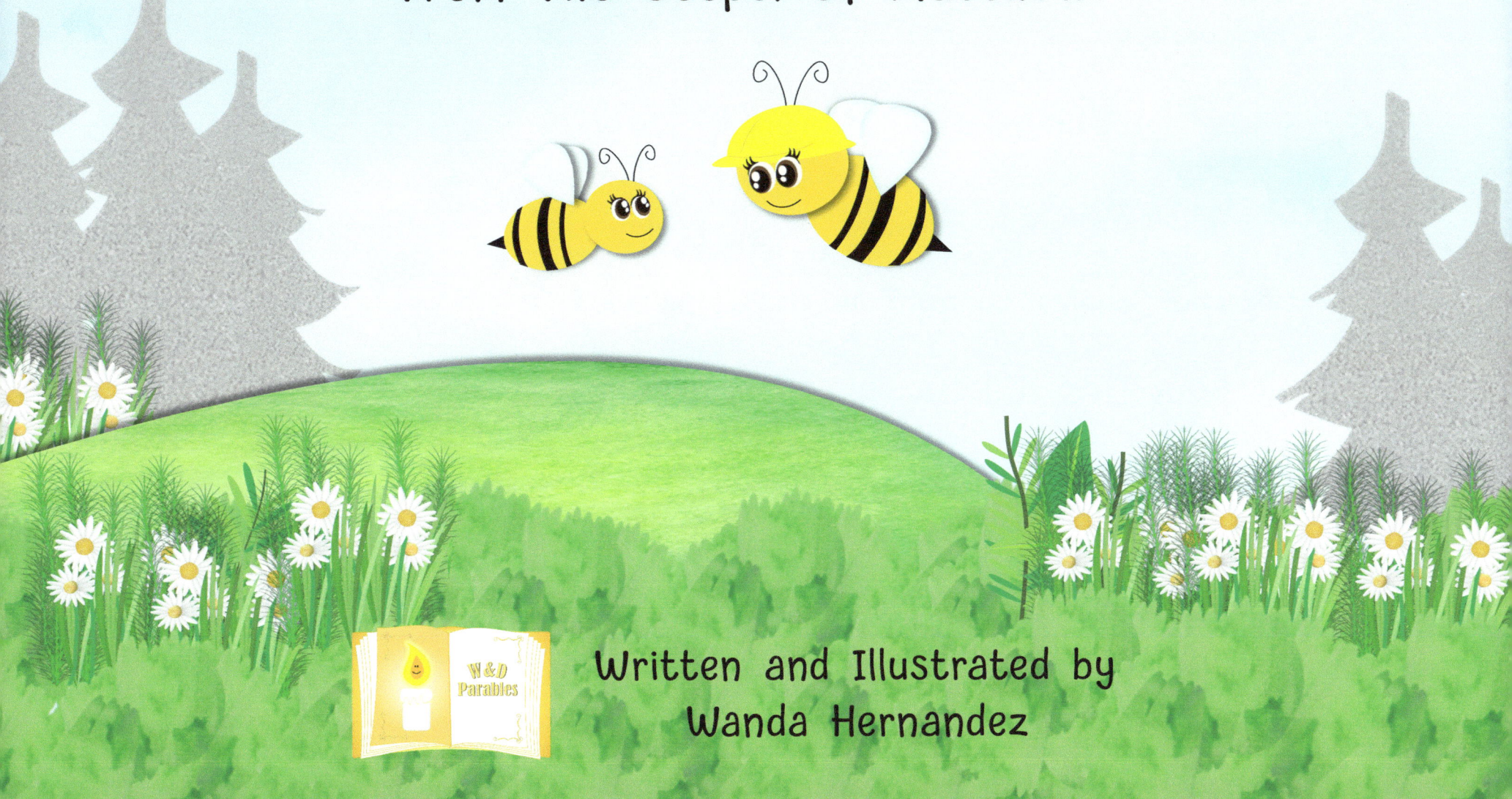

Written and Illustrated by
Wanda Hernandez

Printed in the United States of America

December 2024

Library of Congress Control Number: 2024922957

ISBN 979-8-218-52660-3 (paperback)

Wanda Hernandez
Derby, Connecticut

10 9 8 7 6 5 4 3 2 1

<u>Acknowledgments</u>

I thank the greatest creator who inspired me and taught me how to stretch my gift of creativity, my father God. I also thank Him that He blessed me with this good and perfect gift from above. It is a pleasure to write and draw for His glory. I am truly blessed!

I thank my daughter, Danielle, for all her graphic design consultations.

And special thanks to my friends Martin, Katy, Elizabeth, Dana, Chloe, Monica and Roz for their illustration and editorial advice. I enjoy our monthly meetings very much.

This story is based on Parable Of The Workers In The Vineyard from The Gospel Of Matthew 20:1-16

Scriptures are from The New Century Version bible (NCV), The Living Bible (TLB) and the Good News Translation (GNT).

Early morning, began a new day
and the busy bees have work to do.
They will be rewarded by the queen herself
when their work and the day are through.

Inside the hive,
the bee family work in harmony.
While some bees are nurses,

The workers get food for the family.

Now Big Bee's job is to find more worker bees.
With so many bees to feed there are also extra duties.

Later that morning, Big Bee went out
To find more workers to hire.

They agreed to work and get a reward until the sun set and retired.

At noontime Big Bee found more workers bees.
They said, "Yes!" to the work and reward
And joined her happily.

Early evening, Big Bee went out
and found a small bee at rest.
She said, "Get up and work for a reward.
Be quick! It's almost sunset."

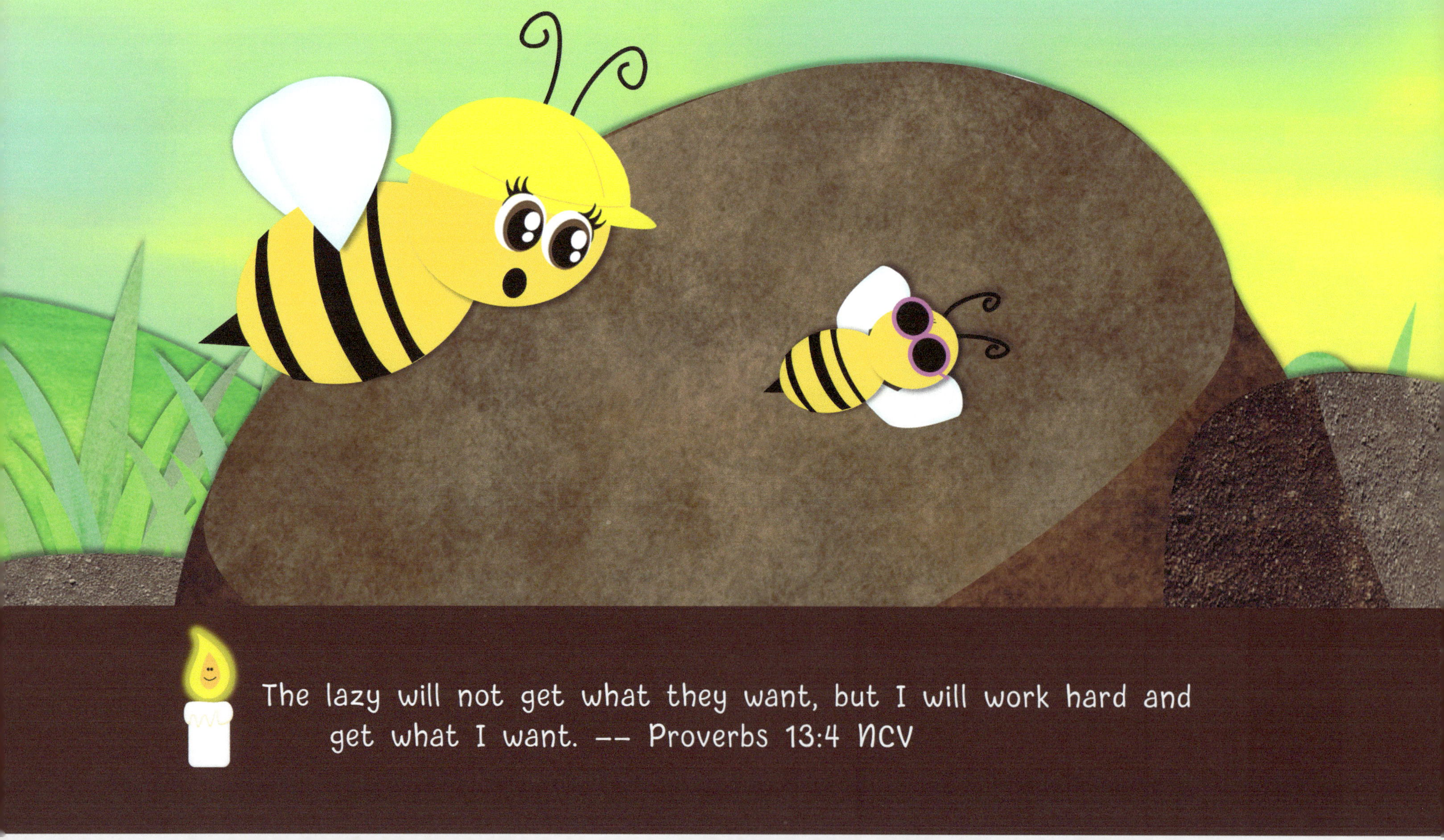

The small bee asked "why should I work?
I am not part of *your* family.
Besides, I'm small and can't do much,"
said this little rude bee.

Big Bee gave this some thought and said,
"I tell you what I will do.
We will work together and *you* keep the reward,
I give it all to you."

The small bee was surprised
And the offer left her confused.
But she thought to herself and said
"I accept, what do I have to lose?"

So they worked together for two hours
and Big Bee spoke only kind words.
The small bee tried to ignore her,
but couldn't help like what she heard.

I will spend time with the wise and will become wise . . . -- Proverbs 13:20 NCV

Later on, the small bee wondered,
"I don't understand this bee.
I am too small to work.
So what does she see in me?"

I trust the LORD with all my heart and will not depend on my own understanding.
—Proverbs 3:5 NCV

The day is over and the bees are back home
to present their work to the queen.
They put in a good days work
and knew the reward it would bring.

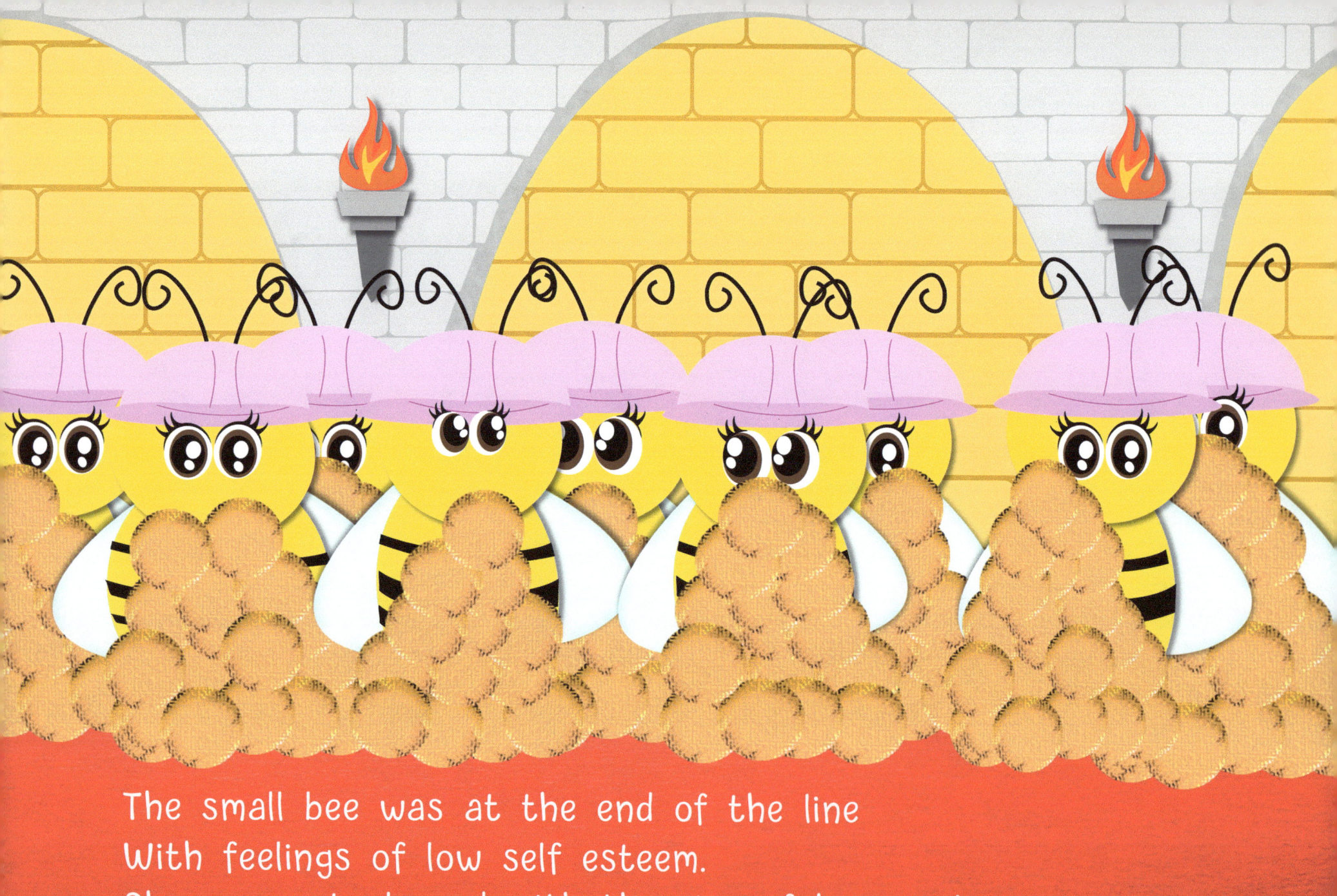

The small bee was at the end of the line
With feelings of low self esteem.
She was not pleased with the size of her work
So she did not want it to be seen.

She thought the queen will never reward her
even though she did her best.
But then Big Bee whispered, "Stand strong and sure,
You belong here just like the rest."

The queen arrived and flew to the end of the line,
making the last in the line now the first.
She said "Thank you for all you have done.
Now it's time to present your work."

The small bee bowed before the queen
and with nervous trembling flew forward.
The queen looked carefully at her work and said . . .

. . . "well done and you get your full reward."

Good news makes me feel better . . . – Proverbs 15:30

The small bee said, "Thank you,
But I did not work much like the other bees."
The queen said, "I judge from the heart
And everyone get what we agreed."

I am a wise person and I speak with understanding . . .   – Proverbs 10:13 NCV

"But my work is not as good as the others,"
the small bee said shyly.
The queen said "but your efforts are great
so welcome to our family!"

The small bee's heart softened at being accepted by her majesty. She felt as good as all the others for the queen showed her grace and mercy.

Happiness makes a person smile.
-- Proverbs 15:13 NCV

WELL DONE!

Big Bee flew to the small bee and asked,
"Well done, how do you feel?"
The small bee said "this is a glorious day.
Today does not seem real.

Tomorrow morning,
can we work together again in the fields?
But this time *you* can keep the reward.
How do you like that deal?"

Big Bee thought for a minute
and kindly said,
"How about we work together
And SHARE the reward instead."

The two bees agreed and Big Bee asked,
"This day has a happy end.
Oh, by the way, what is your name?"

The small bee said, "Just call me friend."

THE END

COME TO JESUS

(confess aloud)

Dear Heavenly father,

I come to you in the name of your son, Jesus, and ask you to forgive me of my sins so that I can be right with you. I believe that Jesus died for my sins and that you raised Him from the dead.

Come into my heart Jesus, to be my Lord and savior. I know I am saved. I am now a child of God in your holy name. Amen.

If I confess that Jesus is Lord and believe that God raised Him from death, I will be saved. for it is by my faith that I am put right with God; it is by my confession that I am saved. – Romans 10:9,10

LET'S TALK ABOUT IT

<u>What Do You Think?</u> Was it fair for the queen to accept the smallest amount of work from the bee that did not work as much as the other bees? Why or why not?
Do you make decisions from the heart?

 **Follow us on YouTube!**
Please give it a like and a comment! We would like to hear from you!

OTHER W&D PARABLES BOOKS AVAILABLE ON AMAZON

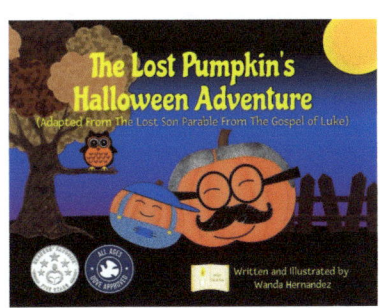 Share a story of God's love to your family on Halloween with The Lost Pumpkin's Halloween Adventures based on The Prodigal Son parable from the Gospel of Luke 15:11–32 of the Holy Bible. Travel with the lost pumpkin from his home to a strange land called foolishness and discover how God's promise to love him no matter what brings him back home again.

 Each of us can do something special and one thing we can all do is speak kind words to each other. Based on Ephesians 4:29 ERV, join a little duckling as she learned that saying good things in times of anger, hopelessness and sorrow can be a blessing to others and a show of love for them.

www.ingramcontent.com/pod-product-compliance
Lightning Source LLC
Chambersburg PA
CBHW040814120626

46547CB00004B/542